HOTSPOTS

SOVIET UNION
WILL PERESTROIKA WORK?

JOHN BRADLEY

A GLOUCESTER PRESS BOOK

Contents

Chapter One
What is *perestroika*? .... p 4

When Gorbachev came to power in 1985, the Soviet Union faced many problems. This chapter outlines them and explains what *perestroika* and *glasnost* are.

Chapter Two
The origins of the Soviet system .... p 10

This covers the history of Russia from Peter the Great through the Russian Revolutions and Stalin's rule to the present.

Chapter Three
Gorbachev's challenge .... p 18

This outlines the difficulties faced by Gorbachev in trying to change the Soviet system.

Chapter Four
Has *perestroika* worked? .... p 24

This assesses Gorbachev's achievements and looks to the future.

Fact file 1
The Soviet Union .... p 28

Fact file 2
The Soviet Economy .... p 30

Fact file 3
The Soviet and US systems .... p 32

Chronology and Glossary .... p 34

Index .... p 36

▷ St Basil's Cathedral is one of Moscow's most famous sights. Its domes are typically Russian. The Soviet Union does not allow much freedom of religion but it has maintained many of the old churches. The cathedral lies on one side of Red Square next to the Kremlin, which contains government buildings.

The Soviet Union has been in existence for over 70 years. Its full name is the Union of Soviet Socialists Republics (USSR). It is made up of 15 republics and contains many different peoples or nationalities. The largest group of people are the Slavs which include Russians, Byelorussians and Ukrainians. Then there are Turkic people, who are descended from the Tatars. Other peoples include the Kurds, Armenians, Estonians, Georgians and even Inuit.

Some 286 million people live in this enormous state. About 116 million work in industry and 10.5 million work in agriculture. Most Soviet people live in flats in towns or cities. The largest city is Moscow which has 8.7 million inhabitants. The next largest city is Leningrad with 4.9 million and then Tashkent and Kiev with more than two million people.

The Soviet Union is one of the largest countries in the world. It covers a sixth of the world's surface – some 22.5 million square kilometres. It stretches 10,900 kilometres from Poland in the west to Alaska in the east. But from north to south it is never more than 4,800 kilometres.

The country consists of six natural zones. To the north there is the tundra of northern Russia and Siberia. In central Russia and Siberia there are mixed forests known as taiga. The world's largest coniferous forest is in the Soviet Union. To the south there are the rich steppes (or grasslands), where wheat is grown. To the southeast there are the desert-like flatlands of Central Asia and in the Far East mountainous areas. The land is rich in oil, gas and coal but these resources are difficult to extract. Most of the north and Siberia suffer from low temperatures and too much moisture. Only the European part and western Siberia have moderate temperatures and moisture. The south is largely desert. This means that it is difficult to grow crops in most of the Soviet Union.

The Soviet Union has a communist system of government. This means the Communist Party and its leaders rule the state. They decide how things should be run from factories to farms and railways. This is different from the democratic system of government we have in the West. For example, in the United States and Western Europe there are several political parties, which electors can choose to be their government. For a long time another difference about the Soviet system was that there was little Western-style freedom. Since Mikhail Gorbachev came to power this has been gradually changing.

What is perestroika?

The Soviet Union faces an enormous number of problems. It has to import food and its people cannot buy the goods they want. Gorbachev, the new Soviet leader, is trying to solve these problems and transform Soviet society.

In 1981 the United States president, Ronald Reagan, described the Soviet Union as an evil empire. He believed that the Soviet communist system was evil. Since the end of the Second World War the Soviet Union and the United States, with very different political and economic systems, have been at loggerheads. The United States has its allies in Western Europe, South America and elsewhere, while the Soviet Union has satellites in Eastern Europe and elsewhere. On many occasions it has looked as if this rivalry between the two countries might lead to war.

In 1948 the Soviet Union and the United States had a major row over the question of access to Berlin. In 1960 the Soviets shot down a US spy plane over the Soviet Union. Two years later the United States insisted the Soviets withdraw their missiles from bases in Cuba. As late as 1983 the Soviets shot down a South Korean airliner thinking it was a spy plane.

Then in March 1985 Mikhail Gorbachev was elected to be the general secretary of the Soviet Communist Party. A month later he stunned everyone by announcing that he wanted peaceful relations with the United States and reform at home.

Gorbachev is the first university educated Soviet leader since Lenin. He was born in 1931 in Stavropol, between the Black and the Caspian Seas. He has always worked for the Communist Party. His appointment as party leader in 1985 was unexpected and he has continued to surprise everyone with his proposals for reforms.

Soviet problems

In 1985 Gorbachev found the country verging on a crisis. For many years the economy had been weak. The Soviet Union was a world superpower alongside the United States. In order to keep up its position huge sums of money had been spent on the armed forces. The Soviet Union also spent money helping communist allies in different parts of the world. The rest of the economy suffered.

Bad organisation and poor harvests meant that for some years the Soviet Union had had to import grain in huge quantities. Consumer goods, such as radio and television sets, cars and refrigerators, were in short supply, and when available were of poor quality. The country was run by the Communist Party whose members lived better than the rest of the people. The system was very corrupt. People paid bribes to officials if they wanted to get something done. The Soviets could put sputniks into space, but could not run the trains or buses on time. The entire Soviet system had to be re-organised: *perestroika* (restructuring) was born.

The birth of *perestroika*

On 23 April 1985 Gorbachev announced a series of measures to save the communist system. *Perestroika* was a long term goal. In the short term, things would not improve. The rationing of meat would continue; food shortages throughout the Soviet Union would cause long queues to grow even longer; people's health would continue to deteriorate because of the neglect of the health system, increased alcoholism and a catastrophic ecological situation; bad housing would persist; and consumer goods would remain scarce.

△ Gorbachev has made a point of breaking with the tradition that Soviet leaders do not talk to ordinary people. He asks about their problems. He is much more open to change than previous leaders.

▷ A Soviet ship taking US wheat on board in a US port. Before 1917 the Soviet Union used to export wheat. In recent years it has had to import huge quantities.

To start with Gorbachev tried out some short term measures but these failed. On 7 May 1985 Gorbachev launched a campaign against drinking alcohol. For years drinking at work had caused accidents and economic losses. The sale of the Russian drink, vodka, was restricted and drinking at work was banned. However these measures did not work. People bought huge amounts of sugar to make their own vodka. Although the consumption of alcohol dropped, by late 1987 it was back at 70 per cent of the pre-1985 level.

Gorbachev realised that he could not change the Soviet system by issuing decrees and launching campaigns. He could only achieve *perestroika* with new methods. One of the key words used by Gorbachev was democratisation – opening up the system so that people's real needs are met. The term *glasnost* was also invented. It means transparency or openness, and has been taken to mean freedom of information and expression.

Glasnost

Glasnost has spread throughout the Soviet Union. Gorbachev has used *glasnost* to improve his position in power. By almost abolishing censorship he was able to discredit incompetent party leaders. They were criticised in the press, on the radio and on television. As a result the Soviet public found out about many cases of corruption including the illegal actions of party leaders in Uzbekistan, and of the former leader's son-in-law in Moscow.

△ In 1988 Brezhnev's son-in-law, Yuri Churbanov, was put on trial for corruption. He had used his position to get bribes from people who hoped he would do them favours.

▽ A helicopter discharges sand onto a burning nuclear reactor. The first test of *glasnost* was the explosion of a nuclear reactor at the Chernobyl power station in April 1986. After a few days' delay, the Soviet authorities told the Soviet people and the world.

In many ways *glasnost* has been more successful than *perestroika* but it still needs to be applied to all aspects of Soviet life. Books have to be more freely available. Communist Party leaders and officials have to be questioned directly by television and newspaper journalists.

The Soviet military machine

Although *glasnost* has uncovered a lot of corruption it has yet to reveal an unsavoury side of Soviet life, the Soviet military and security system. While the military seems to have caused many Soviet economic problems, it has never been challenged by the party or the public. Gorbachev has not yet dared to take the military on. Nonetheless it is known that during the 1970s and 1980s the armed forces spent over 20 per cent of the total amount produced by the country on arms and wars in Afghanistan, Angola and elsewhere.

The Minister of Defence, Marshal Sergei Sokolov, was only sacked in 1987, when a German youth in his Cessna aircraft landed undetected in Red Square in Moscow. This exposed the Soviet military to world-wide ridicule as its sophisticated air defence system failed to intercept the tiny plane. In 1987 Soviet military leaders were very unhappy when Gorbachev signed a treaty with the United States banning medium and short-range nuclear missiles. However, when Gorbachev announced without telling anyone else that the Soviet Union would be reducing the armed forces, several military leaders resigned.

△ Marshal Sergei Sokolov, the Minister of Defence, was fired in May 1987.

▽ The West German youth Mathias Rust at his trial in Moscow. It was his unscheduled flight to the Soviet Union that led to the sacking of several top military leaders. He landed in Red Square.

The Soviet military, therefore, appears to be the greatest stumbling block for *perestroika* and *glasnost*. The West still does not have accurate figures about the Soviet military machine. Until these are available it is difficult to negotiate on Gorbachev's disarmament proposals.

The KGB

The internal security services (KGB) also present an obstacle. The KGB is responsible for keeping political order and dealing with opponents of the Soviet Union. *Glasnost* has only revealed concrete abuses of law by the KGB, such as the case of the torturing and killing of a Donets journalist investigating corruption in the Ukraine. It has not touched upon the KGB's past record, when millions died during the 1930s. There has been no fundamental criticism of this institution, which has enormous economic power. This is based on the extensive network of forced labour or prison camps (*gulags*). Any mention of difficulties in the *gulags* is censored. Some reports about the KGB sending political opponents to mental hospitals for treatment have begun to appear in the Soviet press but it is not clear whether this is still going on.

As long as Gorbachev has to rely on the army and the KGB to maintain political stability, nothing will be done to "democtratise" these two institutions. This illustrates the problems facing Gorbachev's efforts to modernise the Soviet Union: without *perestroika* there will be no modernisation; without *glasnost* there will be no *perestroika*. For his policies to work there must be some democratisation. The people must become involved in modernisation and support the reforms. As long as the army and the KGB keep the people in check, this will not happen.

△ In December 1979 Soviet armed forces invaded Afghanistan. This caused an international outcry and led to bad relations between the Soviet Union and the United States. The United States stopped exporting grain to the Soviet Union and refused to send its athletes to the Olympic Games which were held in Moscow in 1980. The Soviet Union intervened because it wanted to help the ruling Afghan Communist Party. The war dragged on for nearly ten years. The Soviet army could not defeat the opposition from Islamic guerrillas, aided by the United States. Another of Gorbachev's achievements is that he secured the withdrawal of Soviet troops from Afghanistan.

▽ This is a Soviet labour camp, or *gulag*, run by the KGB in Kazakhstan, June 1986. The Soviet Union has from the very beginning used the secret police to silence its critics. In the 1970s the international human rights organisation, Amnesty International, estimated that the Soviet Union had some 10,000 political prisoners in its *gulags*. Men and women who publicly oppose the Communist Party are called dissidents. They were often expelled from schools and universities and lost their jobs. If they continued not to accept the regime, they were sent to a mental hospital or labour camp.

Modernising the Soviet Union

In 1988 Gorbachev told a Communist Party conference "we have underestimated the extent and gravity of the problems". After three years in power he realised that it would take years for the Soviet Union to sort out its economic and political problems.

The task of modernisation is massive. First of all, the old system where the Communist Party had all the power has to be replaced by a new system. If this is to happen, Gorbachev needs the support of the people.

For 60 years the economy has been run by central planning. This means that officials in Moscow tell factories and farms throughout the Soviet Union what they have to produce and how much. For years this has meant that there were shortages of some goods, like shoes, but too many men's suits were being produced. New state laws would give factories greater freedom to decide how they are run. Some might become self-governing public companies. Others might become co-operatives, with the workers having a greater say in how to run the business. Still others might become private companies, run by individuals. In agriculture more families would run their own farms instead of working for the larger state-run farms. All these factories and farms would have to be well run and make money – at present many of them run at a loss.

If the Soviet Union carries out these changes then life will improve for most Soviet people. The Soviet Union might be able to solve the housing and other problems. However the changes may take a long time to work. If it takes too long there will be unrest. If there is a political crisis Gorbachev's reforms will fail.

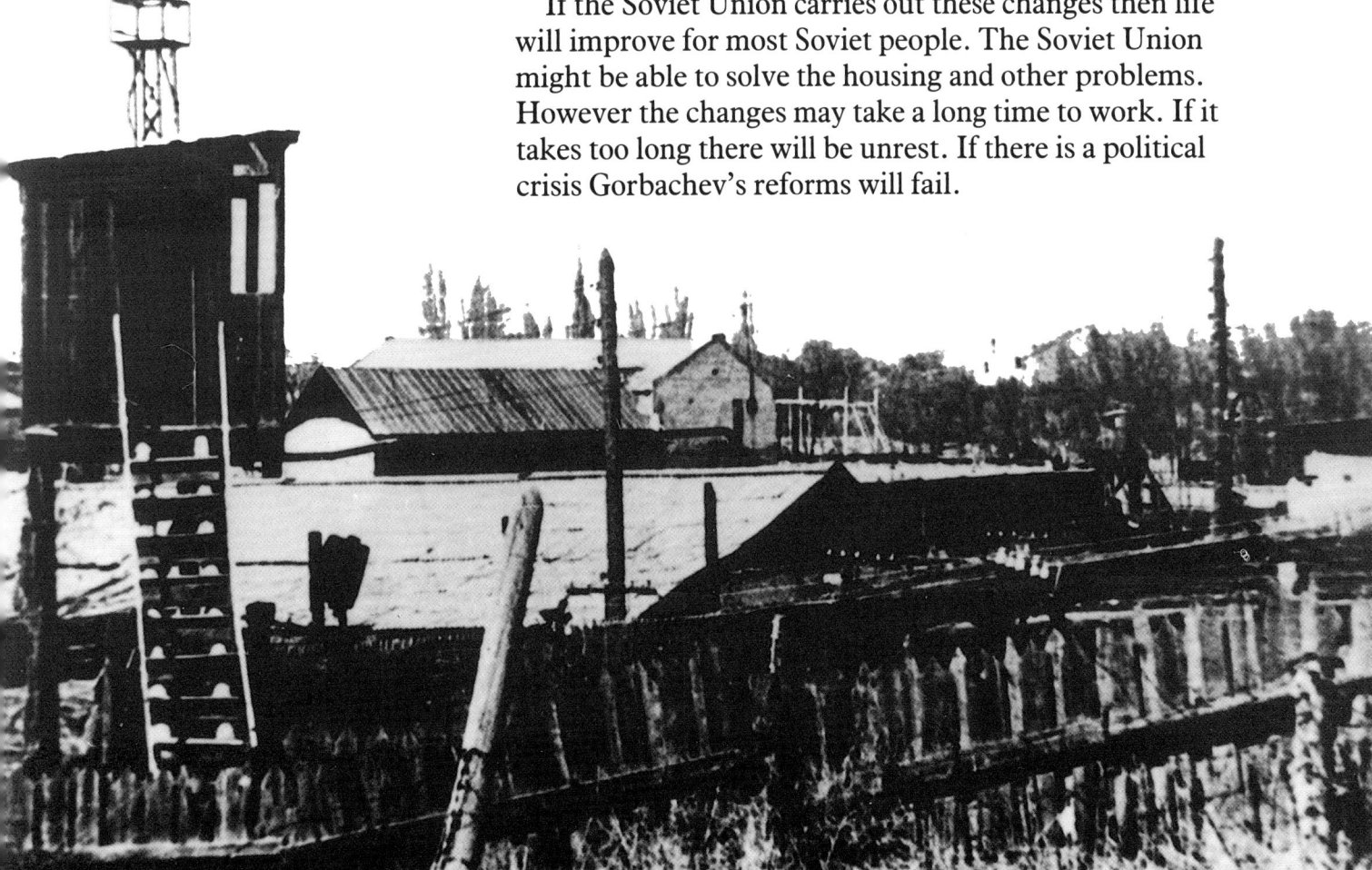

The origins of the Soviet system

The present Soviet system is the result of a long historical process. To understand it we need to look at Russian history and how the Russians have developed their present system.

In the 18th century a Russian king or czar decided to "modernise" Russia. Peter I, known as Peter the Great, was the first Russian ruler to travel throughout Europe. On his travels, he was impressed by the prosperity and stability and by the real power of the European rulers. He came back to Russia with foreign advisers and launched his modernisation drive.

With a stroke of the pen *(ukase)* Peter built his own modern empire. He brought in foreign officers and re-organised the army into modern regiments. Peter created armaments factories. He also set up civil industries (such as shipbuilding, iron casting). He re-organised trade and controlled all trade with foreign countries.

He recruited the most able people to run the country and rewarded them by making them noble. He set up a secret police which was responsible only to himself. Peter's modernisation programme made him the all-powerful ruler of Russia. His plan was to expand Russian territory using his armies, and further increase his power.

The system remained virtually untouched for two centuries and by the time the last czar, Nicholas II, came to

△ Red Army soldiers fighting in 1917. The Bolsheviks succeeded in seizing power in 1917 because their opponents were disunited and because they had the support of the workers in Moscow. It took the Red Army two years of hard fighting to win the Russian Civil War.

power Russia was almost a police state. However the Russian state did not have the resources to run the country as a police state – it was very inefficient. The state could just about survive during peaceful periods, but wars created havoc. In 1904, following the failure in the Russo-Japanese War, there was a revolution.

The March 1917 Revolution

For a very short time, from 1905 to 1914, Russia had a democratic system of government. But the czar still retained a lot of power. Then after three years of fighting in the First World War the czarist system collapsed in March 1917. Russia was in a state of chaos. The army was in mutiny: soldiers were leaving the front line and going home. The police could no longer control anything.

A new government, known as the provisional government, took power and announced that it wanted to improve the previous experiment in democracy. It passed laws trying to set up a democratic system. But the country was in such a state that there were more immediate problems. People had to be fed, clothed and housed.

The October Revolution

The Bolsheviks were a small political party which believed that the old system should be overthrown by a violent revolution so that a system which was fairer to the people could be introduced. Their leader, Vladimir Ulyanov Lenin, saw that it was the right time to try to seize power. In November 1917 they succeeded and Lenin decided to form an entirely new political and economic system, a communist one. Communism is supposed to mean that the people own property and industry not individuals.

◁ Two leaders of the Soviet Union: Josef Stalin (left) next to Lenin in 1917. Lenin spent most of his adult years in exile writing about his ideas. In 1917 he returned to Russia and led the Bolsheviks to power. Stalin worked closely with Lenin and became the leader of the Soviet Union a few years after Lenin's death in 1924.

It soon became obvious that all that Lenin had succeeded in doing was to recreate a police state. He had a secret police (now called *Cheka*) and an army – called the Red Army. It was fighting a civil war against the Bolsheviks' opponents. Lenin used the civil war as an excuse to abolish all political parties, increase the power of the *Cheka*, and seize factories and farms to produce materials for the war effort. This new system was called "war communism" and Lenin was realistic enough to get rid of it as soon as the civil war was over. It resulted in the destruction of life, economic ruin, famine and epidemics.

Lenin's new system
In March 1921 he announced a New Economic Policy (NEP). This meant a return to the old system. It allowed people to trade and profit from their own work so that the country could produce enough grain and goods. Lenin explained that his policies would eventually create a new system which would lead to world revolution and communism. Again it resembled the czarist state: a strong state controlling everything, big standing armies, and an all-powerful secret police. Lenin and the Bolshevik (now called the Communist) Party equalled the state.

As soon as Lenin died, his successors tried to force through their own policies, which were totally different from Lenin's. In the end, Josef Stalin triumphed over his opponents. He succeeded in imposing on the Communist Party and the Soviet Union, his own brand of communism, his own modernisation. More so even than Peter the Great, Stalin was a tyrant who imposed his ideas of modernisation with violence.

Stalin's modernisation programme
Stalin's system was called "socialism in one country". He knew that the Soviet Union was behind the more advanced countries of North America and Europe. He wanted the Soviet Union to become an industrial power rapidly so it could defend itself against any attacks. The first step was to seize the land and create large collective farms. Collectivisation, as this was called, was supposed to produce more grain using fewer people and more machines. Within 10 years, some 98 per cent of Russian farmland had been collectivised.

The other aspect of "socialism in one country" was the modernisation of industry. Two Five-Year Plans were supposed to transform Soviet industry by setting

The Second World War
This is known as the Great Patriotic War in the Soviet Union. It lasted from the invasion of the Soviet Union in June 1941 until the fall of Berlin in May 1945. During that time Moscow was nearly captured by the Germans in December 1941. Leningrad was under siege for three years. The western and southwestern republics were devastated. The Soviet Union lost 20 million people , Poland six million and Germany five million. But the Soviet Union gained a lot of territory including the Baltic republics. It was also able to install communist governments in Eastern Europe.

impossible production targets. Everything was controlled by the Communist Party, which responded to the orders of the supreme leader, Stalin. In time, Stalin succeeded in creating the perfect police state. The secret police, now called NKVD, was given all the power necessary to achieve Stalin's modernisation. It could and did use terror to achieve its objectives. This use of terror became known as the purges.

The combination of Stalin's leadership, the terror of his secret police and genuine revolutionary enthusiasm did achieve a widespread mobilisation of people and resources. The Soviet Union started its industrial revolution, but at great human cost. Millions of lives were lost. Whenever and wherever failure appeared, it was mercilessly "punished" – people disappeared without trace. In time terror became the means of government. It meant Stalin had great personal power over the Communist Party, but it destroyed Soviet agriculture and gravely damaged industrial development. The government had to produce false statistics to demonstrate its success.

Above all the terror damaged the future security of the state. Like Peter the Great, Stalin wanted to increase his territory through military conquest. But the Red Army was ill-equipped to defend itself even from outside threats. In 1941, when war came, Stalin faced another brutal ruler, Adolf Hitler of Germany.

The Second World War

The terror had removed some 40,000 officers from the Red Army. When Hitler's armies invaded the Soviet Union they

△ Soviet troops surrender to the German Army during the Second World War in 1942.

▽ Soviet workers are told about a trial during Stalin's reign of terror in the 1930s. In six years some 18 million people were arrested and millions died.

scored amazing victories. But the Red Army was able to recover from its initial defeats. With the help of the Allies, mainly the United States and Britain, Stalin was able to defeat Hitler after four years of hard struggle. Some 20 million Russians are thought to have died.

By 1945 Stalin had to deal with the reconstruction of the war-damaged Soviet Russia. Before the war many top leaders of the Communist Party had been executed but this had stopped. There were millions of victims of the terror filling up forced labour camps, known as *gulags*. Since neither industry nor agriculture was producing enough, Stalin was planning another terror. Before this happened, he died in March 1953.

After Stalin

Stalin's successors had no idea how to launch a much needed modernisation drive. The countryside was half-destroyed; industry was still far behind that of the United States and Europe; living standards were low; there were millions of prisoners in the *gulags*; and the Soviet Union was cut off from the outside world.

However, the new leaders' ambition was to remove terror from the system, and more particularly from the Communist Party. Led by Nikita Khrushchev, they weakened the secret police and hoped that Stalinism would disappear. By 1956 Khrushchev, now undisputed leader of the Soviet Union, denounced Stalinism and Stalin. He tried to change the Stalinist system by getting the people involved in running things at a local level. The party leaders did not like this and in 1964 Khrushchev retired.

▽ Nikita Khrushchev (foreground) and the Cuban Missile Crisis. The photograph shows Soviet missile bases being built on Cuba in 1962. When the United States found out about the bases, there was almost a nuclear war. Khrushchev lost much prestige with the party leaders.

Leonid Brezhnev was the leader of the Soviet Union for 18 years. His time in power is seen as a period of stagnation. Although there was an increase in the number of consumer goods, the Soviet Union fell further behind the United States and Western Europe in terms of technology and living standards. While he was in power there were many rumours about corruption. Apparently, his daughter collected diamonds and enjoyed an extravagant lifestyle. Brezhnev awarded himself many medals and decorations including Hero of the Soviet Union, Marshal of the Soviet Union, Lenin Peace Prize and Lenin Literary Prize.

The Brezhnev era

Khrushchev's successors, Leonid Brezhnev, Alexei Kosygin and Nikolai Podgorny faced the same problems: an economy that was not working and a very low standard of living for most people. They stopped all the reforms launched by Khrushchev. The three leaders ruled as a collective. They decided that they would solve problems as they appeared by changing the existing system rather than starting a new system. There followed a long period of stagnation when nothing much happened.

With time Brezhnev emerged as the real leader of the three and he takes most of the blame for the stagnation. He was more interested in giving himself all sorts of medals and decorations than solving genuine problems the country had to face.

Nonetheless he did score some successes. Between 1964-74 the Soviet economy did well and as a result living standards went up. Kosygin put through some administrative and economic reforms, which seemed to work. The state put a lot of money into agriculture and that sector improved. However, after ten years of reasonable prosperity economic growth slowed down. By the time of Brezhnev's death in 1982 the Soviet Union was in a recession – a period when there is no economic growth.

Some people argue that the upsurge in prosperity in the first ten years of Brezhnev's leadership was the result of Khrushchev's reforms. Others argue that there were "two Brezhnevs": one up to 1974 and another one (disabled and not taking part in decision making) afterwards.

During his time in power, Brezhnev used repression and the secret police (KGB) became more powerful. A new criminal offence was invented: the slandering of the socialist state and writers were sent to *gulags* for either publishing their poems themselves or abroad. Others were forced to emigrate. Musicians, dancers and writers, such as Alexander Solzhenitsyn, were expelled or went abroad. The result was cultural stagnation.

In fact, the few economic changes Brezhnev agreed to led to economic stagnation. He was in favour of putting money into agriculture. Huge sums were spent on upgrading the soil and on the production of fertilisers and agricultural machines. This proved a waste of money because it was not researched properly. By 1981 the Soviet Union had to import 20-25 per cent of its meat consumption. After disastrous harvests during 1979-81, food queues were a regular sight in the cities.

Industrial decline

The same can be said about Brezhnev's treatment of industry. The Soviet Union continued investing in industry, but always on Stalinist lines – with a view to increasing the number of workers but there was never enough money for machinery. At the same time developments in technology were ignored. In the 1970s when industrial output began to decline the Soviet Union began to buy technology from the West. But these purchases did not stop the industrial decline. They helped the Soviet military industries but had no effect on industry as a whole.

In fact, most of the industrial schemes and projects launched in the Brezhnev era benefited the military and not the people. The army exclusively used the Togliatti car complex, the Kama trucks establishment, the Kama electric power scheme, and the gas pipes from Siberia. As a result the Soviet Union fell behind Japan and fell further behind the West technologically. However, it had produced the world's most powerful military machine.

Military power

Another factor which led to the Brezhnev stagnation was international politics. Brezhnev had no control over the

▽ Cuban troops use Soviet tanks in Angola in 1976. Since Angola achieved independence from Portugese rule in 1975 there has been a civil war. The Soviet and Cuban-backed group, called the MPLA, seized power. It is opposed by two groups, who get some assistance from the United States and South Africa. This shows how the United States and the Soviet Union use other countries to fight against each other.

international situation, but many of his decisions about world affairs made stagnation and decline inevitable. Since 1962, when Khrushchev backed out of the nuclear confrontation with the United States over placing Soviet missiles in Cuba, the Soviet Union was engaged in a major nuclear missile effort.

New industrial centres were set up around Moscow, Leningrad, Chelyabinsk, Dnepropetrovsk, Krasnoyarsk and elsewhere, which in time produced the intercontinental ballistic missiles (SS-16, SS-17 and SS-18s), medium range ballistic missiles (SS-4, SS-5 and SS-20s), as well as missiles launched by nuclear submarines and aircraft. This tremendous effort, which in 15 years consumed some 20 per cent of the total amount the country produced each year, was the main cause of stagnation.

△ Yuri Andropov was the head of the KGB from 1967 to 1982. He became leader of the Communist Party in 1982. He was very ill for most of the years he was in power and used Gorbachev to carry out his policies, such as rooting out corruption.

International problems

In 1975 the Soviet Union's new position as a world superpower was recognised by the whole world in Helsinki, when the Soviet Union, the United States and other countries signed the Helsinki Accords. But this did not help industry: other countries refused to sell technology to the Soviet Union when they realised it was helping it build up its military power.

Another problem was that the Soviet Union had got involved in several regional wars. Soviet troops and advisers were active in Cuba, Mongolia, Ethiopia, Somalia, Egypt, Syria, Iraq, Angola, Mozambique and Afghanistan. A huge army of some 150,000 soldiers tried to hold Afghanistan for the local Communist Party in the face of opposition from Muslim *mujaheddin*. These wars were having a disastrous effect on the Soviet economy.

Brezhnev's successors

Brezhnev died in November 1982 and left a smell of corruption. His successor, KGB chief Yuri Andropov, thought corruption was the only reason for Brezhnev's failures so he launched a vigorous drive against it. However he died before he could realise this was futile.

He was succeeded by the elderly Konstantin Chernenko, who was advised by Gorbachev. But he only lasted a year in office so had no time to make any impact on and improvement in Soviet life. Neither Andropov nor Chernenko thought radical reforms were the answer to Soviet problems. The question was would their successor, the "young" Gorbachev, think differently.

△ Konstantin Chernenko came to power promising to continue Andropov's policies. Gorbachev was his deputy leader and since Chernenko had a lung disease, Gorbachev was able to exercise real power. Chernenko died in March 1985.

Gorbachev's challenge

In March 1985 Gorbachev was elected general secretary of the Soviet Communist Party. He took on the challenge of transforming the Soviet system.

Gorbachev succeeded two elderly party leaders who had both died after a short period in power. It may seem inevitable that the politburo or party leadership finally chose a younger man for the leadership – Gorbachev was 24 years younger than his predecessors. But Gorbachev did not have much support within the politburo.

In fact the politburo wanted another old man, Viktor Grishin, to become general secretary. Grishin was formally proposed by the other "young" man of the politburo, Grigori Romanov. Thus Gorbachev's election to the supreme leadership surprised the whole world, the politburo and the Communist Party included.

At the time of his election, Gorbachev had been in the politburo for almost five years, but the public hardly knew him. At first, he had been put in charge of agriculture and since it had not been doing well, Gorbachev probably decided to keep a low profile. Under Andropov and Chernenko the "young" man got new duties and became more important, number two in the leadership.

Gorbachev started to make himself known both at home and abroad. Significantly it was the British prime minister, Margaret Thatcher, who first focused world attention on the rising "young" man by stating that "she could do business with him". Gorbachev soon proved himself completely different from his predecessors.

△ In November 1987 the Soviet Union celebrated the 70th anniversary of the Russian Revolution.

▷ Gorbachev used *glasnost* to expose the problems of the Soviet system. In this photograph Soviet police show the kind of booty amassed by corrupt party officials. Many of Gorbachev's allies made their names in anti-corruption drives.

Gorbachev in power

As a supreme leader, Gorbachev started out in the same way other leaders had done: he removed all his opponents from the top party positions. Romanov went immediately, the rest gradually. By 1988 six old style leaders had been replaced by Gorbachev's allies and friends.

As well as getting rid of the top leaders, the middle rank leaders in the party were ousted. Some 80 per cent of local party secretaries were replaced as well as the same percentage of state administrators. This traditional treatment of opponents gave no hint of the tremendous changes Gorbachev had in mind.

From the beginning Gorbachev did not want to be a leader like Brezhnev. He would not be happy with the medals and decorations that being in power brought him. Gorbachev wanted real political power. He wanted to be able to exercise all the powers of his office, and be able to put his decisions into practice.

For some time, it had been obvious that the Soviet economy was not working. Therefore, Gorbachev had no choice but to go for fundamental reforms of the Soviet system. The patchy repairs that Brezhnev and Kosygin had put into effect after 1965 could no longer keep the system going. Gorbachev launched his restructuring (*perestroika*) of the system to modernise it.

Putting *perestroika* on the agenda

At first Gorbachev was cautious and did not reveal his intentions even to his fellow leaders. However he introduced new terms to decribe his ideas, such as *perestroika*, *demokratizatsiya* (democratisation), and above all *glasnost* (openness).

Gorbachev knew from the beginning that in order to reverse the economic decline of the Soviet Union, his reforms had to be fundamental and would inevitably provoke opposition. He thought the toughest opposition would come from the state servants or bureaucrats who actually ran the system. There were several million of them so he could not just get rid of them.

They had most to lose from any changes in the system. Gorbachev wanted to use *glasnost* to overcome the bureaucrats' opposition to his reforms. If newspapers, television and radio revealed the incompetence and corruption of the bureaucrats, then the reforms could be put through. *Glasnost* would revive interest in politics and create a more democratic system.

Opposition to reforms

In the next three years, Gorbachev's political skills were fully tested. First of all, he cautiously proposed his reforms. The 27th Communist Party Congress agreed to them in February and March 1986. There was no backlash or opposition, which Gorbachev had feared.

Opposition to his reforms remained passive, though skilful. His measures to encourage the co-operative sector and small businesses were sabotaged when the bureaucrats decided to put a heavy tax on "unearned income". Again *glasnost* rescued the scheme. Journalists uncovered the problem and it was put right after a public outcry.

The same thing happened, when Gorbachev had a law passed which gave businesses greater independence from the ministries which had controlled them in the past. Businesses would draw up their own production plans, obtain the raw materials they needed, elect managers and dismiss them. However the ministries still had the final say on setting prices and production targets. The managers protested and further reforms were put through.

Chernobyl

Then, in April 1986, one of the reactors at a nuclear power station exploded at Chernobyl in the Ukraine. This disaster deeply shocked the Soviet people. It showed up clearly the problems of the Soviet system. Gorbachev decided to exploit this traumatic event and after some hesitation allowed journalists to report on the disaster.

▷ Gorbachev addresses the 19th Communist Party Conference in 1988. This was a major event in Gorbachev's push for *perestroika*. The conference was broadcast live on television and speakers in its debates talked of the desperate need for reform. There was no opposition to Gorbachev's programme and since it was on television it became the people's concern as well as the party's. A new political system was proposed with more than one candidate standing for election to the new body – the Congress of People's Deputies. The new post of executive president was made and Gorbachev was elected to it in May 1989.

▽ Before Gorbachev came to power, pictures of the SS-20 missile were not readily available. This one was photographed in Byelorussia near the Polish border. Shortly afterwards it was removed and destroyed as part of the 1987 arms control agreement.

The *glasnost* campaign

The *glasnost* campaign coincided with that of the *demokratizatsia* of Soviet society. As Gorbachev said "before all the illnesses can be cured, they have to be diagnosed!" The Soviet press, radio and television were allowed to point out the negative side of Soviet life. For example, the pollution of Lake Baikal was widely reported. As a result, official policies had to change.

There was a great deal of questioning by journalists and historians. Stalinism was openly re-examined and condemned in all its aspects, political, cultural and economic. Many political prisoners and prisoners of conscience of the Brezhnev era were released. These changes would have been impossible a few years before.

Foreign policy

The *glasnost* policy produced many useful results for Gorbachev. He wanted peaceful relations with the United States so he could get on with his internal reforms in the Soviet Union. By 1986 the United States became convinced that Gorbachev meant business in the various talks going on about disarmament (known as arms control). But representatives of the United States still said there would be little progress until the Soviets stopped being involved in the regional wars in Afghanistan and Angola and there was more respect for human rights in the Soviet Union.

By December 1987 there was an agreement on the destruction of all medium and short-range missiles in Europe and a clear indication that a treaty on inter-continental ballistic missiles was possible. In 1988 Gorbachev announced the Soviet withdrawal from Afghanistan and by the end of the year it was nearly completed. Then in December 1988 Gorbachev announced that he would be reducing coventional forces. The Soviet Army and Air Force would lose 500,000 troops, 10,000 tanks, 8,500 artillery units and 800 fighter aircraft. These cuts in military spending would free money to go into improving industry.

Arms control will bring economic benefits to the Soviet Union, particularly if it goes with easier trading relations with the United States and Western Europe. The Soviets are still keen to import high technology to modernise industry. Gorbachev was lucky that the Soviet armed forces did not oppose his arms control deals. Feeling confident, he put his reforms before a special, 19th Communist Party Conference for approval. They were accepted.

Nationalist tensions

The conference also discussed an important internal problem: unrest among the different nationalities of the Soviet Union. In Armenia, Georgia, Azerbaijan, Russia itself and above all in the Baltic republics, there have been many demonstrations. It is not at all clear how Gorbachev will tackle this problem. It seems he will follow the same policy he used with the Baltic republics (Latvia, Lithuania and Estonia): firstly, organise a coalition of different political groups, one of which is the local Communist Party. Secondly, allow the coalition to look into the question of greater autonomy or self-government.

Estonia would like to become "free" economically so it can attract foreign money to boost its industry. Both Lithuania and Latvia would like to be able to use the old state flag and make Lithuanian and Latvian the state language instead of Russian. They are not so interested in being independent economically. All these problems are potentially explosive ones. The Estonians and other ethnic groups like the Lithuanians are demonstrating against two centuries of being dominated by Russian czars and the Soviet Union.

▽ In November 1988 there were mass demonstrations in Lithuania to reclaim a national identity. Lithuanian national flags were paraded and people demanded that they be able to use their own language officially. Gorbachev did not use the army to suppress the demonstrations and the unrest continues throughout the Baltic republics.

▽ Hundreds of thousands of Azerbaijani demonstrators marched on the streets of the capital city of Azerbaijan, Baku in November 1988. The unrest between the two republics of Armenia and Azerbaijan over who should rule the region of Nagorno-Karabakh is one of Gorbachev's most serious internal problems. He has handled it very skilfully by not calling in the army. However when he visited Britain in April 1989 local officials called in the army to deal with disturbances in Georgia. Nine people died immediately and some 50 more died later from gas poisoning. It caused great distress and proved that bringing in the army is not the way to solve nationalist unrest.

▽ The elections for the Congress of People's Deputies were held in March and April 1989. Most television and newspaper journalists observing these elections were impressed by the openness of discussions at meetings. This is what Gorbachev was hoping for. If the people put pressure on the party for the reforms to happen, then the party will have to speed things up. The elections showed that the people were unhappy with the party. Some 34 out of 157 regional party secretaries were not elected. The candidates who defeated them were also members of the party but they were standing for a different programme.

Political reforms

The conference agreed to political reforms. It agreed to set up a Congress of People's Deputies. In March 1989 free elections were held for the congress in which many candidates were allowed to stand and people voted using a secret ballot. This was a major step towards greater democracy. Many party leaders lost their seats and critics of the Communist Party were elected.

Conclusion

Gorbachev is the only leader capable of taking the Soviet Union safely through this period of reforms. But he faces many dangers. For the first time in Soviet history, people are being asked to get involved in running their country – for centuries they have been kept under tight control.

Glasnost could lead to much unrest among the Russian people and the other nationalities. In agriculture there is the possibility that the collective farms will not help the reforms. How will the KGB react to the changes? What will happen to the *gulags*? Will the armed forces agree with the reforms when it means they have less money and that they are falling behind the United States? What will happen in cases of national revolts within the Soviet Union and among its allies in Eastern Europe?

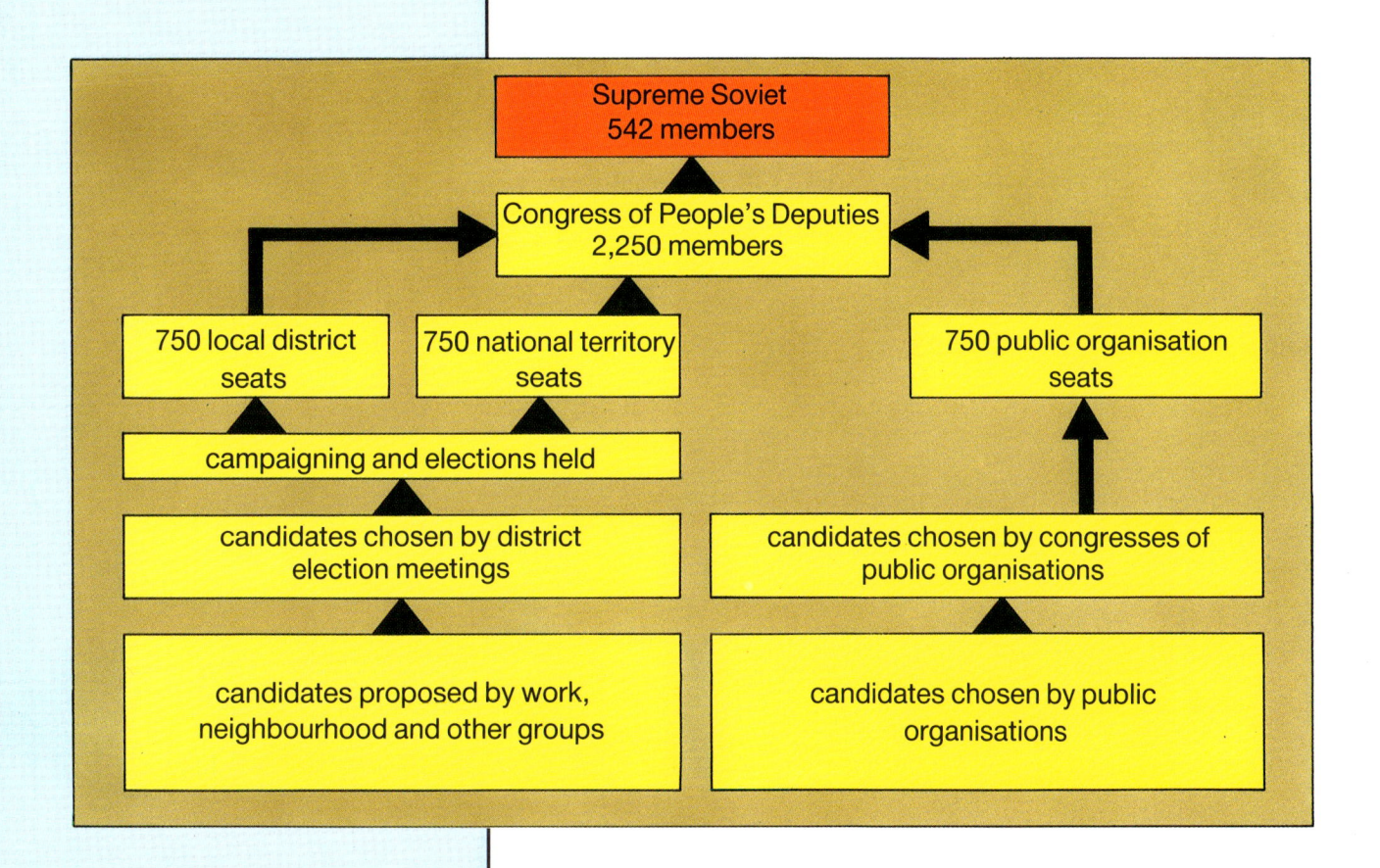

```
                    Supreme Soviet
                     542 members
                          ▲
              Congress of People's Deputies
                     2,250 members
                          ▲
   ┌──────────────┬──────────────┐         ┌──────────────────┐
   │ 750 local    │ 750 national │         │ 750 public       │
   │ district     │ territory    │         │ organisation     │
   │ seats        │ seats        │         │ seats            │
   └──────────────┴──────────────┘         └──────────────────┘
                          ▲                          ▲
           campaigning and elections held
                          ▲
          candidates chosen by district          candidates chosen by congresses of
              election meetings                       public organisations
                          ▲                                  ▲
         candidates proposed by work,              candidates chosen by public
       neighbourhood and other groups                   organisations
```

Has *perestroika* worked?

Four years have passed since Gorbachev became the leader of the Soviet Union. Has perestroika helped to speed up national, social and economic progress?

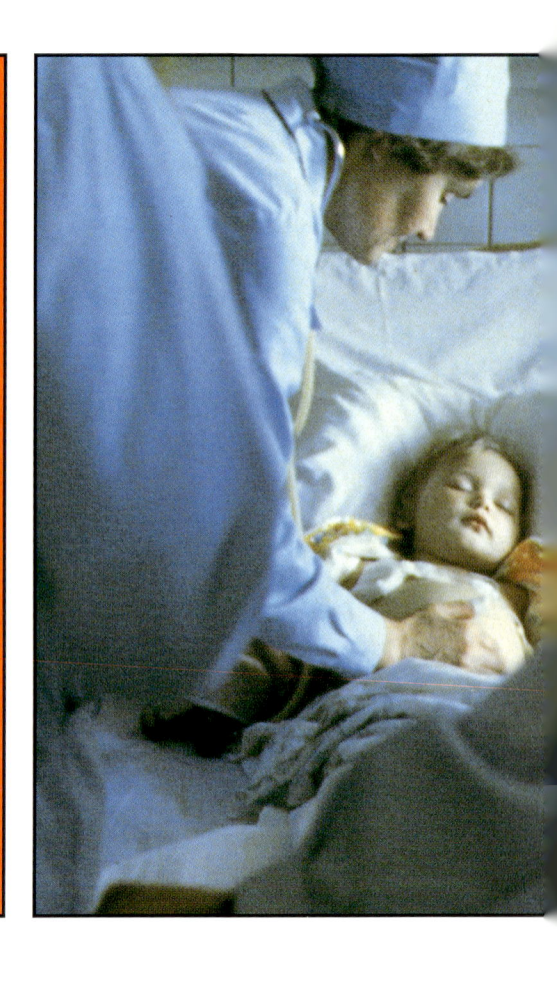

What are the concrete results of *perestroika*? Let us consider the housing problem first. Many people live in overcrowded conditions: several families may share a small flat. If there is no increase in the number of homes built, many people on housing lists will have to wait for their flats until the year 2000. In 1986 the state increased the amount of money it spent on housing by 10 per cent. In 1987, 2.3 million flats were completed, and they were of better quality than in the previous years. If this can be maintained the housing problem will be solved by the 1990s.

△ A children's hospital in Moscow. In some specialist areas Soviet medicine is ahead of the rest of the world but in many others it is far behind.

▽ Agricultural workers on a collective farm. Most families have always had their own plots to grow crops. After Gorbachev's reforms they can lease more land.

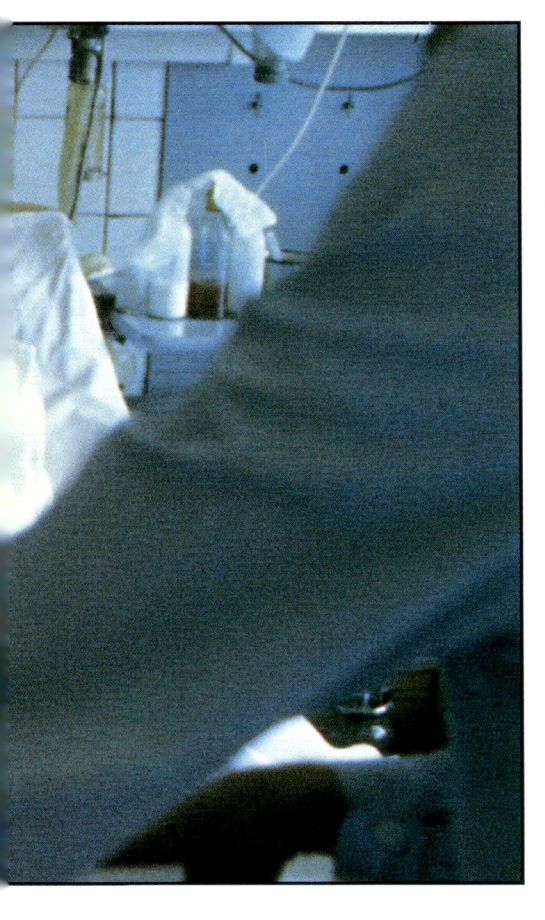

▽ A small co-operative produces the jeans, which most young people in the Soviet Union want to wear.

The food problem

This is more complicated, but it also has to be solved, if life is to improve and *perestroika* is to succeed. Many people never eat vegetables and fruit, because they are not widely available. Food products are of poor quality. This has a bad effect on people's health, particularly the children. Large quantities of meat and grain have to be imported.

Since 1985 the government has put money into producing small tractors and an increasing number of private farmers have entered the market. In 1987 production rose by 9 per cent and there were significant increases in the production of grain, meat and milk.

There has been considerable progress, but the food problem is far from solved. More money will be put into poultry, meat and milk production; further investments will go into building storage facilities, roads, transportation and improving food processing. In addition the distribution of foodstuffs will have to be improved. Once again *perestroika* has only been a partial success so far.

Health care

The health problem is also being solved. In the past only 4 per cent of the total amount produced by the country went into health spending, which is less than half of what other industrialised nations spend. Hospitals are in a poor state, under-equipped and with poor hygiene. In addition doctors' and nurses' salaries are low. Since Gorbachev came to power the salaries of those working in health care have gone up considerably and the health care budget has increased by 25 per cent.

Consumer goods

The availability of consumer goods and everyday services has long been unsatisfactory, but *perestroika* has had positive results. In the first six months of 1988 the production of consumer goods was up by 17 per cent. It will have to go up by 60 per cent in the 1990s if the population's desires are to be satisfied.

This is unlikely but the government is planning to put more money into the production of consumer goods. It is getting rid of nuclear missiles, for example, so that some factories can stop producing military goods and produce washing machines and televisions. Some machines for these new factories will have to be bought abroad. Again the results of *perestroika* in this sector will become apparent only in a few years.

Culture and politics

Thanks to *glasnost* the most positive results of *perestroika* can be seen in the cultural sector. Education has been restructured, teachers salaries increased by 40 per cent and more money is being spent on schools and universities. However there are no new textbooks so teachers have to use the old Stalinist ones (in 1988 history examinations were cancelled for this reason). Historians are writing a more accurate version of Soviet history and are gaining access to papers about Stalin's rule.

Political matters are discussed in public. Freer and more interesting magazines and newspapers, films, television and radio programmes are attracting much larger audiences. All of these changes have certainly enriched Soviet life.

Perestroika has also affected public life and politics. A new political system has been installed and elections were held in March 1989. These were conducted with secret ballots and the electors had a choice of candidates – although most were members of the Communist Party. Many critics of the Soviet system were able to stand and get elected. Andrei Sakharov, the former dissident, was elected to the new Congress of People's Deputies by the Academy of Sciences. Many Communist Party candidates lost.

The quality of life

Thanks to *glasnost* journalists can give us an idea of everyday life in the Soviet Union. Despite *perestroika* it is far from encouraging. Meat and butter, always in short supply, have become even scarcer. Many shops do not have everyday items such as good shoes and toilet paper. Even in Moscow people have to queue for detergents and petrol. Sugar is rationed in most areas of the Soviet Union, though sometimes, inexplicably available in Moscow. Good-quality cheese, coffee, chocolate, fresh fruit, soap, tea and bath towels are also hard to find.

No one can explain these shortages. Some say that this is because the goods do not go into ordinary shops but into the Communist Party shopping networks. Others argue that goods in short supply should be more expensive so that only a few people could afford them. (Price reform was due in 1990, but will be delayed by three years.)

In addition, the quality of Soviet food products, housing, health care and consumer goods is very poor. Thus 10 per cent of the meat that people eat is in fact lard and bone. In any case an average Soviet citizen eats only a third of the amount of meat consumed by a citizen in the United States.

△ Andrei Sakharov was a leading nuclear scientist. During the Brezhnev era he was persecuted by the KGB and sent away from Moscow because he criticised the Soviet system. Under Gorbachev he was set free.

▽ The families of those who died during Stalin's terror put up photographs so that they are not forgotten.

△ Queues outside shops are still a familiar sight in many cities in the Soviet Union. Most women work full time and look after their families. They can spend up to two hours a day queuing at shops for both basic commodities and luxury items. Distribution is sometimes so disorganised that some goods appear almost randomly. This is partly due to shortages but also lack of staff.

Distribution problems

Curiously this unsatisfactory situation is the result of *perestroika*. In the past three years Soviet salaries have risen by 8 per cent. However there has not been any increase in the production of consumer goods, such as television sets, refrigerators, cars and other products. So people use some of their extra money to buy more food. Co-operatives could have produced more consumer goods to fill this gap. But, for some unknown reason, they have been forbidden to sell certain items, such as jewellery.

In 1989, the Communist Party newspaper *Pravda* published a story about the shortages. It showed television sets, champagne bottles and heaps of vegetables piled up at various railway stations in Moscow. *Pravda* even hinted that sabotage by handlers and transport workers might be the cause of the problem. However, the Moscow city manager rejected the sabotage idea and blamed the chaos on the "usual disorganisation".

Thus while *perestroika* is solving many Soviet short and long term problems, it is not doing much about the "usual disorganisation". If it fails to solve it, then Gorbachev may fall and the new Soviet order may fall with him. This could mean an end to hopes for world peace. Gorbachev's success is the whole world's concern and we may see the day when the Western world has to help out the Soviet Union financially for the sake of world peace.

THE SOVIET UNION

The Soviet Union is made up of 15 independent republics. The sheer size of the Soviet Union means that the republics are self-governing. It would be difficult for the central government in Moscow to run the republics from such a great distance. Within the 15 republics there live some 160 different nationalities and there are 131 languages spoken within the Soviet Union. There is very little feeling among all these different people that they are part of the same country. This is a major problem.

The Russian Republic
This is the largest republic and is composed of Russia and Siberia. It stretches from Leningrad to Vladivostok – a mere 9,329 km. The Russians have been deeply influenced by the East and have developed their own religion based on Greek Orthodox – known as the Russian Orthodox Church.

The Ukrainian Republic
The Ukrainians are the second largest nationality and have their own language and customs. They have a long history dating back to the Middle Ages and were independent for a few months in 1917-18. It is rich with thriving agriculture and industry.

The Byelorussian Republic
Byelorussia has its own language. Its economy is not as rich as the Ukrainian one but its lumber and textile industry are important.

The Uzbek Republic
The Uzbeks are the largest of the Turkic nationalities, which are all muslim. Uzbekistan borders on Afghanistan. It is the main cotton-producing area and also has large textile and chemical industries.

The Kazakh Republic
The Kazakhs are also muslim. Kazakhstan is a desert north of Kirghiz and Uzbekistan. Many Russians and Ukrainians have settled in Kazakhstan.

The Turkmen Republic
Turkmenistan is another desert region.

The Kirghiz Republic
This republic borders onto Sinkiang in China. For centuries the Kirghiz have been nomads, tending their horses in mountain pastures.

The Tadzhik Republic
The Tadzhiks are a Persian people – related to the Iranians. They are also muslims. Their main work is farming, looking after animals and mining.

The Azerbaijan Republic
This lies on the other side of the Caspian Sea. The Azerbaijanis are another Turkic muslim group. Within its borders lies the autonomous area of Nagorno-Karabakh, in which many Armenians live. There has been much unrest because Armenia would like to govern this area. Azerbaijan is very fertile. Cotton, rice, tea, fruit and fish are farmed. Oil is found at Baku.

The Georgian Republic
Stalin came from Georgia. It lies in the Caucasus Mountains and is a rich and colourful area. Tbilisi has manganese deposits. Tea, grapes and citrus fruits grow there abundantly. It follows very independent policies.

The Armenian Republic
Armenia has a long tradition which includes persecution by the Russians and Turks. In 1989 it suffered a catastrophic earthquake which flattened several cities.

The Lithuanian Republic
Before the Second World War Lithuania was an independent state. Its people are Baltic and closely related to the Poles. Most are Roman Catholic.

The Latvian Republic
Latvia was also an independent state before 1945. Its people are overwhelmingly Lutheran.

The Estonian Republic
The Estonians are related to the Finns, Hungarians and Turks. Its language is based on Finnish and its people are Lutheran.

The Moldavian Republic
Moldavia borders on Romania. It used to be called Bessarabia and its people are mainly Romanians.

	Republic	Population
	The Russian Republic	146,400,000
	The Ukrainian Republic	51,400,000
	The Uzbek Republic	19,569,000
	The Kazakh Republic	16,470,000
	The Byelorussian Republic	10,141,000
	The Azerbaijan Republic	6,921,000
	The Georgian Republic	5,297,000
	The Tadzhik Republic	4,969,000
	The Kirghiz Republic	4,238,000
	The Moldavian Republic	4,224,000
	The Lithuanian Republic	3,682,000
	The Armenian Republic	3,459,000
	The Turkhmen Republic	3,459,000
	The Latvian Republic	2,673,000
	The Estonian Republic	1,571,000

THE SOVIET ECONOMY

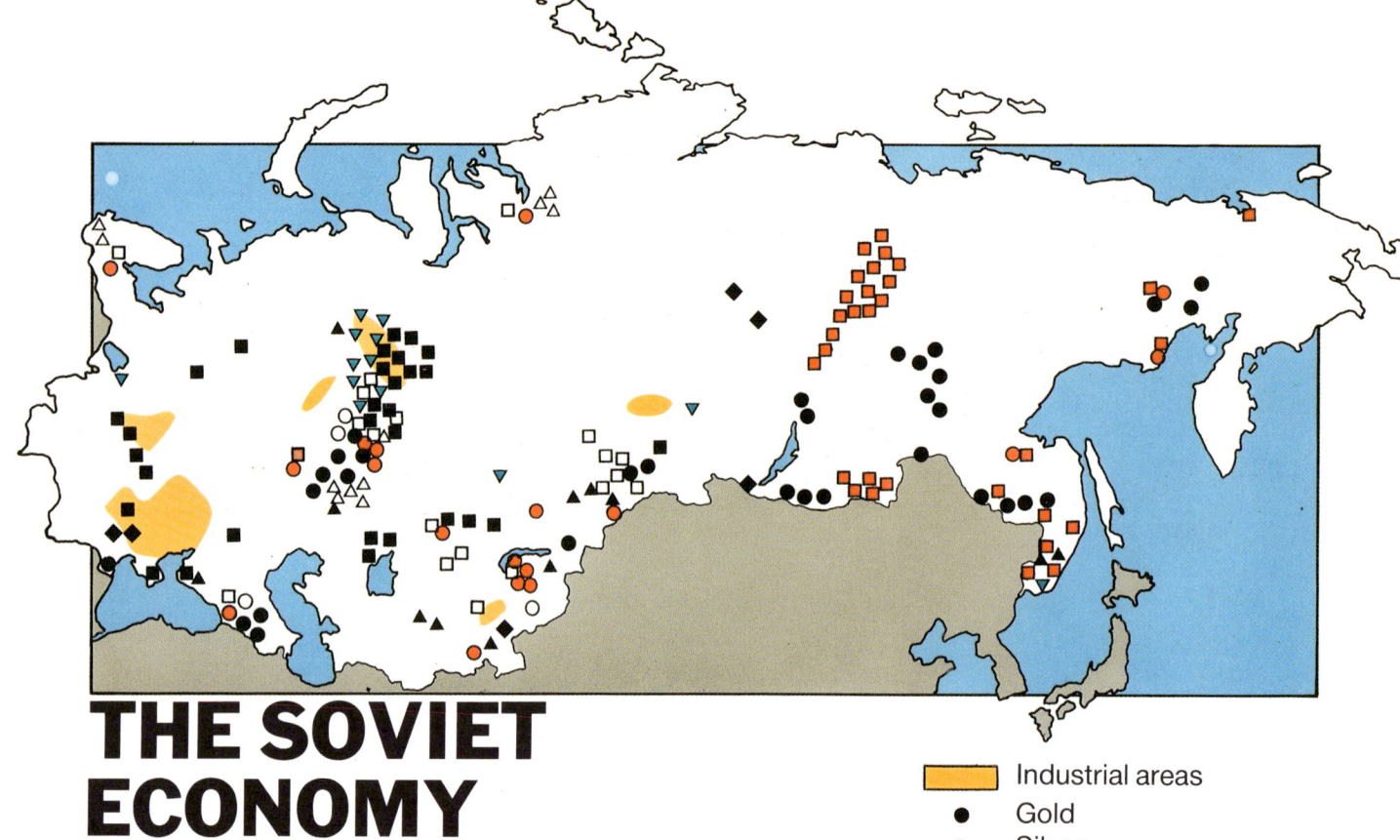

The Soviet Union is a country of enormous natural resources. It has the world's largest reserves of iron ore and manganese. There are huge stocks of bauxite (from which aluminium is made), copper, silver and gold. It is a leading producer of coal and oil and has some of the largest reserves of natural gas. The Soviet Union is the world's second largest agricultural producer (after the United States). It has the world's largest coniferous forests and is the second most important fishing country.

Economic problems
With all these advantages its economy is not working. Every year the Soviet budget is in deficit, that is, the government spends more than it receives.

Its people have a low standard of living compared with other countries in Europe. Prices of housing and food are kept low by the government, which means everyone can eat. However it also means that even though Soviet workers are not paid much, the people have a lot of money saved.

There is a shortage of consumer goods, such as televisions, cars, washing machines, radios. So there is nothing for the people to spend their money on. There is not enough housing so people live in overcrowded conditions.

Workers on farms and in factories do not produce as much as workers in countries like the United States and the Netherlands.

Central planning
Under the rule of the Communist Party, the Soviet Union has an economic system run by central planning. All factories and farms are owned by the state. Each factory and farm is told by the ministry in Moscow how much it must produce. The produce is bought by the ministry, which also provides all the raw materials.

There are many problems with this system. The factories

Legend:
- Industrial areas
- ● Gold
- ○ Silver
- ▲ Lead
- □ Zinc
- ■ Iron ore
- △ Nickel
- ▽ Bauxite
- ● Copper
- ◆ Uranium
- ■ Tin

△ The map shows that the Soviet Union produces a lot of metals. They are found mainly in the Ural mountains and in Siberia.

Oil and natural gas
The Soviet Union has vast reserves of oil and natural gas. It has always exported its oil so that it can buy foreign goods. In the 1970s large deposits of both were discovered in Siberia, which gave a much needed boost to the economy. Recently a pipeline was built across Siberia to Western Europe so that gas can be transported and sold more easily.

🟨	Grain farming
🟧	Livestock farming
🟧	Dairy farming
🟪	Mixed farming
⬛	Intensive farming
🟩	Nomadic herding
⬜	No agriculture
⬛▶◀	Major fishing ground
⬜	Other countries

△ The map shows the different kinds of land use in the Soviet Union. Much of Siberia is so inhospitable that nothing will grow. The grain belt extends from the Ukraine and Georgia through Russia.

do not produce what people want or need. Their managers must produce what they are told to. If the people want washing machines they have to wait because the stainless steel is being used to make tanks. Also if the ministry forgets to put in an order for shoes then no shoes will be produced that year.

Because the factories have to produce a fixed monthly total they work in spurts – work is slack at the beginning of the month and frantic at the end. If the factory meets the target it has been set, the managers and workers get extra pay. The fact that the goods are badly produced, do not work or are of bad quality is irrelevant.

Workers do not feel responsible for putting in a full day's work because they will get paid regardless of their work. It is difficult for a factory manager to sack workers but it is easy for a worker to leave a boring job. Many factories do not have enough skilled workers. Drinking vodka at work has long been regarded a major problem. There are accidents at work and people off sick because of drinking. Many of the machines used in factories and farms are old and out of date.

There are also problems in getting goods to the right place at the right time. Many state shops, where the price of goods are fixed, have empty shelves.

Gorbachev's reforms
Gorbachev wants to make the Soviet economy more efficient. He wants workers and managers to feel more responsible for the work they are doing. Factories have to make a profit, that is, they must make more money than they spend. Factory managers will be allowed to order the materials they need, plan their production, develop new products, sell their products and expand.

In agriculture families are encouraged to take leases of 50 years or more on land. They will then produce crops and sell them. They will keep any profit they make and pass on their lease to their children.

In service industries, such as hairdressing, restaurants and driving taxis, people are being encouraged to set up on their own. People are also encouraged to set up co-operatives where people share the responsibility for running the business. About two million people are now thought to be working like this.

THE SOVIET AND US SYSTEM

President
is elected by the people for four years. He is the head of the executive. He can serve two four-year terms.

Cabinet
is chosen by the president. It includes the heads of departments, such as, Defense, Treasury etc.

Congress
is made up of two houses, the Senate and the House of Representatives. It can change any law proposed by the president.

Senate
Each state elects two members, called senators. They are elected for six years. Every two years there are elections.

House of Representatives
is composed of 435 representatives, who serve for two years. They serve local districts and represent local interests.

Supreme Court
is made up of judges, chosen by the president and approved by the Senate. They decide on problems in the law. They can declare that a law is not acceptable.

The US system
In the United States there is a presidential system of government. The president and his advisers (the Cabinet) carry out government policy. The president is elected by the people every four years and has considerable power.

However to make sure the president's power is not too great there is a separate legislature. This is the law-making body, known as Congress. If the president wants a new law passed it has to be approved by Congress.

Congress is made up of two elected bodies, the Senate and the House of Representatives. Every year the president has to get the Congress' approval of the budget – that is how the government will spend its money.

If the president does not agree with a law passed by Congress, he can veto it. The Supreme Court interprets the law and can decide on disagreements between Congress and the president.

What was the old system in the Soviet Union?
Gorbachev wants to reform the Soviet system. Under the old system the Communist Party controlled everything. About nine per cent of the Soviet people were members of the party. Voters were only allowed to vote for party members.

The party's top body, the politburo, made all the important decisions – who was the leader, the ministers and all other important matters. The law-making body, the Supreme Soviet, had no power and only agreed to laws put before it.

The new restructured system
It is thought to be based on the US system and is extremely complicated. Gorbachev wants to break the state power of the Communist Party and have a more democratic system.

The first step is to make elections more open. A new body, the People's Congress of Deputies, has been set up. It has 2,250 deputies. Some 750 are elected by local districts, 750 by national territories, 750 by public organisations, such as the Academy of Science and the Communist Party.

Anyone can be proposed as a candidate for election. He or she has to be accepted by more than half the numbers present at a meeting of 500 people and another pre-election meeting. In practice most of the candidates are members of the Communist Party.

Deputies have to receive more than 50 per cent of votes. Another new feature of the system is that electors vote in secret – they put their marked papers in a ballot box.

The Congress of People's Deputies
It has some real power. The Congress will meet once a year. It elects the new-style president. It elects 542 of its members to the Supreme Soviet.

At the moment it is not clear exactly what the Congress will do. It will decide how the new Soviet system will work. It will also decide who will sit in the Constitutional Court. It will be a more democratic body than the ones under the previous system. It will have public debates and will be shown on television.

The president

The new role of president is similar to that of the US president. The president is the head of the executive, which includes the Council of Ministers. The executive carries out government policy. It controls relations with other countries, how money is spent, the country's defence, health and many other matters.

Gorbachev is the first president to have been elected under this new system. He can only serve for a maximum of two five-year terms. He is not elected by the people but by the Congress of People's Deputies. He runs foreign policy, is the commander-in-chief of the armed forces and signs all new laws.

The Council of Ministers

The chief minister, or prime minister, is proposed by the president and approved by the Supreme Soviet. The prime minister proposes the ministers for such departments as transport, health, old people, education, social security and other important matters. The ministers carry out government policy.

The Supreme Soviet

This is supposed to be like the US Congress. It makes laws and acts as a check on the actions of the president and ministers. The two houses are the Soviet of the Union and the Soviet of Nationalities.

It is elected by the Congress of People's Deputies and is made up of 542 members – 271 in each chamber. Its membership will be rotated every two years.

The Supreme Soviet approves the appointment of the prime minister and the Council of Ministers. It can call a minister to appear before it for questioning. It also has special committees to look into particular problems. The committees can call ministers and ministry officials.

The Soviet of Nationalities will have the difficult task of working on the problems existing between different republics and nationalities within the Soviet Union. For many years these have been put down with force. Now there are different demands from different groups who will be able to voice them.

The Constitutional Court

As in the US system there is a court which examines any problems arising between different parts of the government. If the Supreme Soviet does not agree with a minister the matter would go to this court. The court is elected by the Congress of People's Deputies.

Will there be other parties?

At the moment there are no other political parties in the Soviet Union. Gorbachev said in March 1989 "Other parties by themselves will not solve the problems." So it is not clear that the Communist Party will allow other parties to organise.

This means that within the party there are people with very different views. For example, in the Baltic republics there are party members who support the old system and others who want their countries to have more independence.

President
is elected by the Congress. He is the head of the executive and can serve for up to ten years.

Council of Ministers
is approved by the Supreme Soviet. There are 50 ministers, responsible for transport, health etc.

Supreme Soviet
is made up of the Soviet of the Union and the Soviet of Nationalities.

Soviet of the Union
has 271 members. They are elected by the Congress.

Soviet of Nationalities
has 271 members. It is the senior body and represents the republics.

Congress of People's Deputies
This new body is made up of 2,250 deputies. It elects the President and the Supreme Soviet.

Constitutional Court
It is called a committee but acts as a law court. It is elected by the Congress of People's Deputies. It looks at election problems and matters of law.

CHRONOLOGY

The Kingdom of Russia started in the 9th century on the banks of the River Dnieper. For centuries it was subject to raids and invasions from the east. In the 14th century it reformed on the banks of the River Moskva. From the 18th century onwards its history has been one of massive expansion until it reached its present borders after 1945. In 1917 the communists came to power. Since then the country has been called the Soviet Union.

1682-1725 Peter the Great modernises Russia and brings in European ideas.

1861 Alexander II frees the serfs. Most Russian peasants continue to live in terrible poverty. He is murdered by revolutionaries.

1894 Nicholas II becomes czar of Russia. He is weak and ineffective.

1905 Russia loses the war against Japan and there is a revolution. Nicholas II regains power.

1914 The First World War begins. Russia loses several battles and several million soldiers die over the next three years.

1917 The army mutinies. The czar resigns and a provisional government takes over. In October the Bolsheviks seize power.

1918 Lenin makes peace with Germany. The Civil War begins with the Bolshevik Red Army fighting its opponents, the White Army.

1920 The Civil War ends with victory for the Bolsheviks.

1921 The New Economic Policy is adopted.

1922 Widespread famines in the Soviet Union.

1924 Lenin dies and there is a struggle between his successors. Stalin emerges victorious.

1925 The party adopts the slogan "communism in one country".

1928 The first Five Year Plan is announced by Stalin. He starts his reign of terror.

1941 German armies invade the Soviet Union. The Soviet Union becomes an ally of the United States in December.

1945 Soviet armies defeat Germany in the East and take Berlin. Soviet troops occupy Eastern Europe and eventually East Germany, Czechoslovakia, Poland, Hungary, Romania, Bulgaria and Yugoslavia become communist satellites of the Soviet Union.

1946 The United States and Soviet Union disagree over the future of Europe. A Cold War between them begins.

1953 Stalin dies. Khrushchev becomes leader after four years of shared rule.

1962 The Cuban Missile Crisis. The United States nearly goes to war with the Soviet Union, which has built missile bases on Cuba. The Soviet Union agrees to withdraw the missiles placed in its bases.

1964 Khrushchev is replaced by Brezhnev, Kosygin and Podgorny.

1969 The Soviet Union and the United States begin talks on arms control at Helsinki.

1972 Brezhnev and US President Nixon sign arms control agreements at Moscow.

1975 Helsinki Accords signed.

1979 New agreement on arms control between Soviet Union and the United States; Soviet forces invade Afghanistan.

1982 Brezhnev dies; Andropov succeeds him.

1984 Andropov dies; Chernenko succeeds him.

1985 Chernenko dies; Gorbachev becomes the new leader of the Soviet Union.

1986 The 27th Party Congress approves Gorbachev's policies.

1987 Gorbachev has a summit with President Reagan and signs an arms control treaty.

1988 Reagan meets Gorbachev in Moscow; 19th Communist Party Conference approves all the new proposals; Soviet army withdraws from Afghanistan.

1989 General election held.

GLOSSARY

Bolsheviks The group of communists led by Lenin, who seized power in the Soviet Union in 1917. The word means "majority" in Russian.

Collectivisation Stalin seized all farms in private hands and made collective farms, or *kolkhoz*. There are about 40,000 today.

Communism A system which believes that wealth should be divided among all the people and not be just in the hands of the rich.

Communist Party It is the only party recognised in the Soviet Union. About 10 per cent of the people belong to it. Anyone who wants an important job needs to be a member. Members of the party can shop in special party shops and get many privileges.

Congress of People's Deputies This is the body of representatives elected for the first time in March 1989. Its membership is elected by the people and by official groups.

Council of Ministers The ministers are approved by the Supreme Soviet. There are over 50 ministries in the Soviet Union.

Democracy This is a system of government in which the people are involved in running the country. In European Community countries and the United States democracy means that people can choose their government from several different political parties or different candidates. Elections are held every few years. It comes from the Greek word meaning "people's rule".

Elections This is the choosing of a leader or representative by a system of voting. In European Community countries and the United States this means choosing from several candidates. It comes from the Latin word meaning "to choose".

First World War A war fought between 1914 to 1918. It was fought by Germany and Austria against Britain, France, Russia and the United States.

Five-Year Plan In 1928 Stalin produced the first one. It was to industrialise the Soviet Union.

KGB The State Committee on Security, the Soviet secret police.

New Economic Policy Lenin set up this system which allowed land and industry to remain in the hands of individual owners.

Pravda This is the newspaper published by the Communist Party. The word means "truth".

President Gorbachev is the first elected president. He was elected by the Congress of People's Deputies.

Politburo This is the small group of leading Communist Party members who control the government. The word means "political bureau".

Second World War A war fought between 1939 and 1945, mainly in Europe and the Far East, which involved many different countries. The principal opponents were the Axis Powers consisting of Germany, Italy and Japan. They were fighting the Allies: the United States, Britain, France and the Soviet Union.

Soviet The first soviets were groups of workers, sailors, soldiers and peasants who took over power in 1905 and 1917.

Supreme Soviet This is the law-making body of the Soviet Union. It is elected from the membership of the Congress of People's Deputies. It consists of the Soviet of the Union and the Soviet of Nationalities.

Taiga The forest zone of Siberia, which contains a mixture of coniferous and deciduous trees.

Tundra The treeless zone in the north of the Soviet Union.

Ukase A decree or instruction, issued with the stroke of a pen. The Russian czars ruled by issuing *ukases*.

Vodka The Russian national drink, made from the cereal rye.

Vote This is how people show who they are choosing in an election. It comes from the Latin word meaning a "wish".

War Communism The policy followed by the Bolsheviks after they seized power in 1917. They seized factories and land in order to produce what was necessary to fight in the Civil War.

INDEX

Afghanistan 7, 8, 17, 21, 28
agriculture 3, 5, 9, 12-15, 18, 23-25, 30, 31
Air Force 21
Alaska 3
alcoholism 5, 6, 31
Andropov, Yuri 17, 18
Angola 7, 16, 17, 21
Armenian Republic 3, 22, 29
arms control 20, 21
army 7, 8, 10-12, 16, 21, 22
autonomy 22
Azerbaijan Republic 22, 29

Baltic republics 12, 22, 33
Beria, Lavrenty 14
Bolsheviks 10-12, 35
Brezhnev, Leonid 6, 15-17, 19, 21, 26
Britain 14, 22
bureaucrats 19, 20
Byelorussian Republic 3, 28

censorship 6, 8
central planning 3, 9, 12, 30, 31
Cheka 12
Chelyabinsk 17
Chernenko, Konstantin 17, 18
Chernobyl power station 6, 20
China 29
Churbanov, Yuri 6
cities 3
co-operatives 9, 20, 24, 27, 31
collectivisation 12, 23, 24, 35
Communist Party 3-5, 8, 9, 12-14, 18, 19, 23, 26, 27, 30, 32, 33, 35
Communist Party Conference, 19th 20, 21, 22
Communist Party Congress, 27th 20
communist system 3-5, 11, 35
Congress of People's Deputies 20, 23, 26, 33, 35
Constitutional Committee 33
consumer goods 5, 25-27, 30, 31
conventional forces 21
corruption 5-8, 17-19
Council of Ministers 33, 35
criticism 6-8
Cuba 16, 17
Cuban Missile Crisis 14, 17
culture 26
czarist system 10-12, 22

destalinisation 19
democracy 3, 6, 8, 11, 23, 26, 32, 33, 35
disarmament 7, 8

dissidents 8
distribution 25, 27, 31
Dnepropetrovsk 17
Eastern Europe 4, 12, 23
ecology 5, 21
economy 3, 5-7, 9, 11, 12, 14-17, 19, 21, 30, 31
education 24, 26
Egypt 17
elections 3, 23, 26, 32, 33, 35
emigration 15
Estonian Republic 3, 22, 29
Ethiopia 17
everyday life 26

factories 31
First World War 11, 35
Five-Year Plans 12, 35
food 25-27, 30
foreign policy 4, 5, 7, 16, 17, 21

geography 3, 29, 30
Georgian Republic 3, 22, 29
glasnost 6-8, 18-21, 23, 26
glasnost campaign 21
Gorbachev, Mikhail 3-7, 9, 17-23, 26, 27, 31-33
Great Patriotic War 12
Grishin, Viktor 18
gulags 8, 14, 15, 23

health 5, 24-26
Helsinki Accords 17
Hitler, Adolf 13, 14
housing 3, 5, 9, 14, 24, 26, 30
human rights 21

industry 3, 9, 10, 12-14, 16, 17, 21, 25, 28, 30, 31
intellectuals 21
intercontinental ballistic missiles 17, 21
Iraq 17

Japan 16

Kazakh Republic 8, 28
KGB 8, 15, 17, 23, 26, 35
Khrushchev, Nikita 14, 15, 17, 19
Kiev 3
Kirghiz Republic 29
Kosygin, Alexei 15, 19
Krasnoyarsk 17
Kremlin 2
Kurds 3

labour discipline 19
Latvian Republic 22, 29

Lenin, Vladimir Ulyanov 4, 11, 12
Leningrad 3, 12, 17, 28
Lithuanian Republic 22, 29

March Revolution (1917) 11
media 6, 7, 19-21, 23, 26
mental hospitals 8
military power 7, 8, 16, 17, 19
military spending 5, 21, 25
modernisation 8-10, 12-14, 19
Mujaheddin 17
Moldavian Republic 29
Mongolia 17
Moscow 3, 7-10, 12, 17, 24, 26, 27, 30
Mozambique 17
MPLA 16

Nagorno-Karabakh 22, 29
nationalism 22, 23
nationalities 3, 28, 29
natural resources 3, 30
New Economic Policy (NEP) 12, 35
Nicholas II 10
NKVD 13
nuclear weapons 7, 17, 21

October Revolution (1917) 11
Olympic Games 8
opposition to reforms 19, 20
party leaders 6, 7, 14, 19, 23, 26, 32
peace 4, 7, 27
perestroika 4-8, 19, 20, 24-27
Peter I 10, 12, 13
Podgorny, Nikolai 15
Poland 3
police state 11-13
politburo 18, 32, 35
political prisoners 8, 21
political reform 20, 23, 26, 32, 33
political system 32-33
Pravda 27, 35
presidential system 32
prices 26, 30, 31
provisional government 11

Reagan, Ronald 4
Red Army 10, 12-14
Red Square 2, 7
reform 14, 15, 19, 31
regional wars 17
religion 2, 28, 29
republics 3, 28-29
Romania 29
Romanov, Grigori 18, 19
Russian Civil War 10, 12

Russian Republic 3, 28
Russian Revolution 10, 11, 18
Russo-Japanese War 11
Rust, Mathias 7

Sakharov, Andrei 26
salaries 27
Second World War 12-14, 29, 35
secret police 10-15
self-management 9, 20, 31
short-range missiles 21
shortages 5, 9, 25-27, 30
Siberia 3, 28
Slavs 3
socialism in one country 12
Sokolov, Marshal Sergei 7
Solzhenitsyn, Alexander 15
Somalia 17
South Africa 16
Soviets 35
space programme 5
St Basil's Cathedral 2
stagnation 17
Stalin, Josef 11, 12, 13, 14, 26, 29
steppes 3
superpower 5, 17
Supreme Soviet 32, 33, 35
Syria 17

Tadzhik Republic 29
taiga 3, 35
Tatars 3
Tashkent 3
Tbilisi 29
technology 16, 17, 21
terror 13, 14
Thatcher, Margaret 18
Togliatti cars 16
trade 10
tundra 35
Turkic peoples 3, 28, 29
Turkmen Republic 29

ukase 10, 35
Ukrainian Republic 3, 8, 28
United States 3-5, 7, 8, 14, 16, 17, 21, 23, 26, 32
Uzbek Republic 6, 28

Vladivostok 28
vodka 6, 35

war communism 12, 35
Western Europe 4, 21
workers 31

Photographic credits

Cover and pages 6t, 8, 10, 11, 12, 14r, 15, 16, 17 both, 18-19, 20, 24, 25 and 27: Rex Features; pages 2-3, 4-5, 5, 6b, 7 both, 9, 19, 21, 24-25, 26, 26-27 and back cover: Frank Spooner Agency; pages 13 and 14l: Popperfoto.